Poems I Wrote in College

By
Lauren Cidell

Transcript: Poems I Wrote in College
© 2016 by Lauren Cidell

Purple Turkey
Second Edition, 2020

ISBN: 978-0-9997515-3-4

Dedicated to the Sinsinawa Dominican Sisters, with special thanks to those from whom I was privileged to learn:

Sister Jeanne Crapo
Sister Clemente Davlin
Sister Marci Hermesdorf
Sister Melissa Waters

Special Thanks as well to Professor Mary Scott Simpson for helping me to refine my voice.

Contents

Foreword

I went from a public high school in excess of 3500 students to a small liberal arts Catholic college of 250, including graduate schools. As part of freshman orientation I went on a bus tour of Chicago. I'd lived near the city all my life but I'd only ever seen small parts of it.

I remember at one point we stopped to stretch our legs on one of the bridges over the Chicago River. One moment I was gazing down at the water, the next I was scrambling for pen and paper. To this day I feel that I didn't write "River Town" so much as I wrote it down.

Over the next four years I would be fortunate enough to experience similar moments. I spent the fall semester of my junior year in a study abroad program in the United Kingdom. Included was a ten day tour of England and Scotland. I wrote most of the poems from that time during that tour.

And now I offer them to you the reader. I hope you enjoy reading them as much as I enjoyed writing them.

--Lauren Cidell
February 29, 2016

River Town

Spanned by bridges great and plain,
Lined with buildings large and small,
Waters churning, ever green,
Traversed by boats both short and tall,
The great Chicago River flows
Down from the locks all through the year.
The current speeds and then recedes
A stream of love and hate and fear.
From the uptowns to Downtown
It goes along without a care.
It was in Chicagoland
Before the town was ever there.
Toss in a coin and make a wish.
Sweet town Chicago day and night
Carries the River at its heart
Reflecting all the city's light.

Transcendence

If kings and queens from long ago
Could come back to us from the past,
If knights and monks and artisans
Could see the wonders that still last,
If philosophers and scientists
Could gather in one big salon
Could cross the boundaries of Time
And have debates the whole day long,
If all languages were the same
If all great boundaries were crossed,
If Understanding came to all
If nothing more was ever lost,
We'd be one people once again:
The people of the Planet Earth
One land, one race, one government
With all the rights we have at birth
Just think of all that we could learn
And all the things that we could teach
If we could pass beyond our present state
Nothing could be beyond our reach

Fly Away Home

He made his nest in the Tree of Life,
Which bears fruit and blossoms always.
He drew strength from the Heart of the Tree,
And passed it one to all he knew.
He closed himself to no one,
But ever gave and gave.
A guide on the path between Self and Divine.
His pilgrimage now complete,
He crosses from one to the next
Carrying the Love and Light he received while
        in the flesh
Gone, but not Forgotten,
His spirit still touches us in Death as it did in
        Life.

The Cardinal has left his nest
And flown on to his new Home
Rest In Peace, Cardinal Bernadin

Mirror Mantra

There is power in the Mirror.
The Mirror is the crystallization of Truth.
Nothing can hide from it.

We all have a Mirror within us.
One that we can use whenever we need it.
Anything at comes into our life,
We can hold up to our Mirror.
They will see themselves in it.
All that is Bright and Truly Beautiful will not
     be stopped.
All that is Dark and Truly Ugly will be
     repelled and fly away from the Truth.

Our Mirror is our Shield and our Guardian.
It protects us from the Demons and Shadows.
It allows the Light and Warmth of Love and
     Life into our Being

Such is the power of the Mirror.

At the End of the Road

There is Peace.
There is Comfort.
There is Rest.

These are the meadows I ran through.
That is the pond where I played in the
      summer.
These are the trees I climbed and sat in
      dreaming, cradled in the blossoms and
      branches.
There is the Barn where I found Love in so
      many miracle ways.
There is the House that was and is yet my
      Home.
I can see them all in my mind.
I hold them all in my heart.
And all of them lie just around the bends of
      this muddy old byway.
All down at the end of the road.

Sojourn

On the Journey of Life there are many stops.
We travel from world to world,
Even as the tourist goes from one sight to the
      next,
Collecting memories all the while.

I spent my earliest years in a world wither
      community was slowly dying
Friends and family journeyed on before me,
      called to new abodes.
Strangers came and upset the balance I had
      known.

I left it for a world of people, people, so many
      people.
Faces and names blended together into a
      meaningless swirl that grew wider and
      deeper.
And flew stayed long enough to grow a root.

I left it for a world of opulence.
Stately trees, formal gardens, and grand old
      houses provide the perfect façade for
      modern comfort and convenience.
Hestia and hobbits have blessed this place.

I can visit the first two worlds.
Traces of me linger in them yet.
And the soil from their lands still clings to my
      feet.

But I do not belong there anymore.

There are shade and support in these trees.
There are shelter and safety in these stones.
There are knowledge and understanding in the
      minds of these people.
And friendship and warmth in their hearts.

The letters on the envelope tell the truth quite
      clearly:
Until I am called on to another,
This world is my home.

Sex as a Form of Meditation

Our Bodies are Magnets
Filled with both Matter and Energy.
First we must unsheathe the Magnet.
Ready to project, ready to receive
Feel the Pulse of your own Inner Energy
Equal and Opposite to your own.
Feel the two Pulses draw to each other.
Two Halves fusing into a Whole
Your breathing, your heartbeats, your bio-
      rhythms synchronize.
You have achieved a state of Oneness
In a Perfect Fit.
The Agonies of Separation transform into the
      Ecstasies of Union.
Forming a bond of Love that nothing can break
Until you let go.
Slowly drawing away
Dispelling back into selves,
But near, or far apart,
You can always feel the Magnetic Power and
      Pull of the Pulse.

Cleansing By Fire

Alone in a room
Sitting in the dark
Surrounded by ghosts and despair

A spark kindles.
The candle casts its small glow,
The fire dances on the wick,
Driving away the shadows,
Consuming all the bad feelings
Even as it nibbles away at the dark blue wax.

In the heart of the flame,
I can see them.
All my anxieties burning away.
Dwindling down as the candle does,
Leaving nothing but smoke.

Lingering Spirit

She returned to her old haunts,
The Ghost of Lincoln-Way
To see her friends and enemies,
That cold October day.
Visiting and listening,
To be back she was glad.
But looking deep into her eyes,
You could see she was sad.
She'd graduated long ago,
A mere four months before;
And although she was welcomed back,
She belonged there no more.
No one noticed when she left,
That cold October day.
She went to find a warmer place,
The Ghost of Lincoln-Way.

Mac

He's always there when I need him.
I know he'll never leave.
He always does as I ask,
Although he continues to beat me at chess.
He remembers everything I tell him,
And I know just how to turn him on.
He sings to me,
Checks my spelling,
Helps me to communicate myself to others,
And all of this without any fuss,
Except when he's sick or bogged down.
Always charged and ready,
I don't know what I'd do without my Mac.

Respect

Honor the body,
And you honor the soul.
Someone who hits you
Cannot love you.
She eats poorly,
Starves her spirit.
He who drinks the night away
Poisons his essence with every drop.
Disturb not the dead,
That their rest be your own.
Cleanse the flesh,
And purify the mind.
Our souls are gods
With our bodies for temples
Revere them.

Immaterialism

Furs, jewelry, perfumes, candy, roses
All of these are worthless
Expensive, perhaps, but worthless
How can a mink coat keep you warmer than
      the arms of your beloved?
Can the glitter of shaped rock and metal rival
      the sparkle of loving eyes?
A false musk cannot entice true
And kisses taste best when not made of
      chocolate
How can a flower that will quickly wither
      symbolize a lasting love?
Don't present me with gift-wrapped affections
My devotion doesn't come with a price tag

The Power of Religion

Strength comes from faith.
There are no questions,
And no confusion,
Only Truth.
Knowledge without the need for
        Understanding
Facts and figures are inconsequential.
All that matters is what you believe.
You need not reason,
Only accept what is
What your inner being tells you.
Follow your heart,
And you can't go wrong.
Nothing truly bad will ever happen to you
As long as you keep the faith.

Sister Melissa

If she weren't a nun,
She'd be a grandma.
She has enough love to embrace the whole
        world
Without excluding anybody.
Whoever meets her becomes a friend.
Always ready to listen, to help, to comfort.
Teacher and helper
Ready to seek the Truth in all its forms
She has found God's Love
And wishes to share it with everybody.
A shining example of Christ's ministry

Taper

The candle is the perfect metaphor for life.
It comes in many sizes, shapes, and colors
As it burns, it consumes,
But it also provides light and warmth,
If only for a little while.
Unlit, a candle is pretty, but useless.
A darkened light serves no purpose.
A hidden light offers nothing.
Yet though a candle will burn itself out,
A life can shine forever.

First Kiss

No romance, no tenderness,
Only unadulterated lust.
The fact that I can't remember his name or
     face well,
Just goes to show how worthless he was.
I dreamed of a prince,
But received a beast.
I knew not the difference
Till it was too late.
The waters have been sullied
The flower petals are worn and withered
I can never go back,
But must carry the thorn forever in my heart.

Manna for the Soul

Break my bones,
And I will heal.
Tear my flesh,
And I will heal.
Spill my blood,
And I will heal.
Break my heart,
And I will die.

Love is the only true reason for living.
Love gets us up in the morning,
And gentles us to sleep at night.
Love is the food of the soul.
The one thing we must have to give our lives
        substance.
Let each one have their mate,
And find comfort and joy in each other.
There is no greater glory or higher honor.
To lose love is to lose the very essence of life.
Though our bodies may survive,
Our souls cannot often endure to be without
        love.

Break my bones,
And I will heal.
Tear my flesh,
And I will heal.
Spill my blood,
And I will heal.
Break my heart,
And I will die.

C'est La Vie

As it has been,
So it is now,
So it shall be for all Time

We live by learning.
We build by burning.
For every action there is an equal and opposite
        reaction.
So that which is created need must be destroy.
Either by accident,
Or by design.

For such is the Natural Way,
The Way of the Universe,
The great mixture and melding of Order and
        Chaos.

Modern Day Babel

New York has the Empire State Building.
Chicago has the Sears Tower[*].
London has Big Ben.
D.C. has the Washington Monument.

From these great heights,
We look down on the rest of the world.
We build taller buildings all the time.
Our spires mimic the mountains,
Rising up to touch Heaven,
Taking us farther away from our dominion on
      Earth,
As we seek to join God in Heaven

---

[*] This poem was written prior to the 2009 name change to Willis Tower.

Cyberspace

Enter a Universe that no one can see,
But that everyone can experience.
A world where Man and Machine are the same
A world of minds and energy
There are no boundaries.
No one is excluded.
Language is not a barrier.
True reality melts away,
Replaced by the virtual

World in a Box

"And in other news…"
"Now a word from our sponsor."
"Derek, you can't leave me!"
"Doctor, will she make it?"
"You'll never take me alive!"
"Here's the pitch. Strike One!"
"What's up, Doc?"
"Darling, I love you."
"You have the right to remain silent."
"Pat, I'd like to solve the puzzle."

God put Humankind on this Earth to take care
     of it.
We are meant to exist in harmony with all
     living beings.
The mountains, rivers, plains, and forests
     belong to us all.
We can all share in the beauty and majesty of
     the glory of Creation.

And all we have to do is click to the Nature
     Channel.

Auschwitz

The silence is filled with the ghosts of echoes:
The agonizing screams of the dying,
The harsh profanities of their Nazi captors,
The periodic whistles of the trains,
And the constant roar of the crematory fires.
The ground is stained with blood and ash.
The winds that carried the black snow and
      smoke are now stilled.
The officers and soldiers of the camp are long-
      gone.
The Allied liberators have since returned
      home.
The survivors have fled seeking new haven,
A place to rebuild as their ancestors have done
      since Abraham.
But here and now stands a living monument,
One that shows the terrible sins that people
      can commit against people.
Here and there people leave flowers to honor
      the memories of those who did not
      survive,
But who found escape in death, men, women,
      and children.

The buildings, the fences, all of it remains just
      as it was,
So that we will never forget those who died
      and those who killed.
It is not easy to remember,
But it is our duty.
We must work to remember, work to learn,
      and work to heal.
For as the sign on the gate says:
Work will make you free.

Arlington

The rolling fields are evenly planted with
     uniform white stones.
The eternal flame provides small warmth for
     Kennedy's mourners.
Even on the quietest day you can hear the click
     and march of the Unknown Guard.
Everyone here has given his life for fifty stars
     and thirteen stripes.
Five-star generals, flight team leaders,
     flagship admirals, non-com privates
All have found peace here.
They threw themselves under Tyr's chariot
     wheels
For the sake of Duty, Honor, Country
To preserve Truth, Justice, and the American
     Way.
How many didn't have to?

Questions of a Pacifist

How many mothers' sons have died?
How many widows and orphans cried?
How many homes have been destroyed?
How many souls cast into the void?
How many bombs have discharged their fire?
Making the death-toll higher and higher?
How many have died for a long-lost country?
How many more must die to be free?
How many times can we blow up the Earth?
How many deaths fore every one birth?
How many women's hearts must break?
How many tombs will the gravemaker make?
How many years will you fight in your war?
Tell me how much longer till we are no more?

Femme Power

No matter how hard an Amazon fights,
She is never defeated.
No matter how high a Valkyrie flies,
She never falls.
No matter how deep a Mermaid swims,
She never drowns.
No matter how far a Unicorn wanders,
She is never lost.
No matter how many times a Phoenix
        combusts,
She is never destroyed.
No matter how hard an Angel is tempted,
She never sins.
No matter how bad a Mother's children are,
She never stops caring.
No matter how low a Lady sinks,
She never loses her dignity.
And no matter how a Woman looks,
She is always beautiful.

Fairest of God's Creations

No matter how a woman looks
She is always beautiful
She has the natural beauty bestowed on all
     women by God
She has the beauty of her share in the Glory of
     Creation
She has the beauty of the Eternal Essence of
     the First Mother
She has the beauty that springs from the
     depths of a warm and loving heart
She has the beauty of the purity she has held
     and will return to
She has the beauty of the strength gained from
     works of love
She has the beauty of her sistership with all
     women
A bond that goes beyond the flesh
Consider the women you see every day
They're your friends, family, and lovers
Cherish them in your heart
And know that they are always beautiful

Goddess Queen

I am the quintessence of Woman
Empress of the heart and soul
Standing on my pedestal for all to admire

It's lonely up here
I have no equal
And no one to talk to
All are willing to gaze in worship
But no one dares to touch
I am cherished and adored
Honored and revered
But never truly loved

Is it any wonder I am made of stone?
And not flesh and blood

Crone in the Park

You can tell she knows the pain
That is the widow's grief.
The cheerfulness of summertide
Gave her no rest or relief.
She has come back to this park
To see their special place,
But on the old wood bench beside her
Is only empty space.
Autumn has made its debut
With its Midas' touch of gold.
It serves only to remind her
That now she is quite old.
She will rest a moment more;
She has no wish to leave.
When winter comes she will go home,
And continue there to grieve

Autumn Advent

Tired now the sleepy world
Prepares itself to rest.
The trees have shed the finery
In which they have been dressed.
Winter brings from Fairyland
The Keepers of the Frost
Summer's golden jubilees
Now must pay the cost.
These leaves are patches on the quilt
That blanket lawn and lane
But when old Bacchus blows his horn
They'll rise to dance again.

Persephone's Return

Today she leaves her fearsome groom,
None other than the Lord of Gloom.
Zephyrus flies to spread the word,
Passed along by every bird.
The Mother ceases then to weep,
And rouses Terra from her sleep.
The world puts on its finest green,
A shade as such is rarely seen.
Lady Iris shows her sign:
The coming of the Girl Divine.
Hermes, messenger of Fate,
Meets his cousin at the gate,
To bring her swift to old Demeter,
Who prepares all mortalkind to meet her.
Phoebus shines in all his glory,
As priestesses retell the story.
Children come outside to play
No one mourns this holiday.
The gods all smile from the skies
And in the air dance butterflies.
Hope grins within Pandora's Box
On this the Vernal Equinox.

Zodiac New Year

The stars have once more made their run,
Even as Earth went round the Sun.
The dual Pisces fish swim on.
The Aquarian waterman is gone.
The Aries Ram moves into place
With its stern yet gentle face.
The Time of Water now is past.
The Time of Wind has come at last,
Bringing with it springly airs,
A coming sign of summer fairs.
When its time to shine is full,
The Ram gives way unto the Bull.
High in the sky through shine and rain,
The stars shall do their dance again.

Bonfire of Love Letters

Total Destruction
No evidence remains that it ever happened.
The white turns black.
The words are obliterated.
Piece by piece goes up in smoke.
Lost for all time
Even as the memories are consumed and
      absorbed.
That which creates also destroys.
Until nothing remains but a pile of ashes
And a cloud of already fading smoke.

Waltz with Satan

I will never forget that Halloween night
When I danced with the Devil in the full
     moon's light.
I was in my bedroom, bored and alone,
Just sitting and staring at my silent phone.

Everyone else was out having fun,
And Halloween Night had only begun.
I heard a knock and looked out in the hall,
But I could see nobody there at all.

Closing the door I saw in my room,
A dark handsome man dressed up like a
     groom.
He held out his hand, "May I have this dance?"
It was like a scene from a harlequin romance.

Caught by surprise, I gasped looking down
To see that my sweats had turned into a gown.
I took his hand, and he drew me near
And although I should have, I felt no fear.

I then felt quite dizzy as though I would fall,
When we were transported to the Black Forest
     Ball.
Around us danced witches, wizards, and
     ghouls,
Vampires, monsters, gremlins, and fools.

The music came down to us from the high
    trees.
The heat of the dancers was cooled by the
    breeze.
I gazed up into my partner's dark eyes.
And what I saw there gave me much surprise

The coldness of evil was deep in his gaze.
I read there the cruelty of his wicked ways.
To him I was nothing, just some silly girl
Who lived all alone in a fantasy world.

All of a sudden, my partner was gone.
The sun was just coming up over the lawn.
I was back in the dorm with the new day
    begun.
My roommate was back from her evening of
    fun.

Reality hit in the form of a spark.
I cannot continue to dance in the dark.
I can have all the best that the world has to
    give.
All I must do is go out there and live.
I will never forget that Halloween night,
When I danced with the Devil in the full
    moon's light.

Dementia

True Insanity is the willful refusal to
      acknowledge the chaos and misery of
      existence.
The butterfly is the happiest creature in the
      world
Because it is completely unable to contemplate
      this tragedy.
The Fools are the wisest people of around.
They acknowledge but don't accept.
For them ignorance is bliss
Because ignorance is innocence,
And innocence is the paradisiacal state of mind
      that we pursue,
And despise the Fools because it comes to
      them naturally.

True Depression is the acceptance of the chaos
      and misery of existence.
We accept it, but we seek escape anyway.
Drugs, liquor, sex, food, material possessions,
      physical luxury whether real or
      fantasized—
All of these offer the chance to escape
Even religion can be abused in this way.
We either absolve ourselves from all
      responsibility,

Or pile it on adding to a growing mountain of
     troubles.
We compete for sympathy and attention,
Wallowing with perverted pride in our
     sufferings,
Exalting in the role of Victim.
Not realizing that the melody of the Song of
     Sorrows is always the same,
No matter what the words are in our own little
     verses.

True Joy is the ability not to let misery taint
     you.
That doesn't mean isolating yourself or seeking
     escape.
But instead realizing that joy and misery are
     irrevocably link.
For they always exist in the presence of each
     other:
For someone to be accepted, someone must be
     rejected.
To have a winner there must be a loser.
The First indicates the Last.

In order that the good may glow in Heaven the
     wicked must burn in Hell.
The two extremes meet because they must.
Without Chaos to tame, Order becomes
     meaningless.
If there is no Darkness, why turn on the Light?

Burning Pockets

SETI spends millions of dollars listening for a
    signal that may never come.
The military spends just as much building
    weapons they may never use.
Corporate America can match that amount
    developing products they may never sell.
Hollywood pours more of the same into a movie
    that may bomb.
In the meantime people starve.
Hospitals must turn away the uninsured.
Crooks go unpunished because the system
    can't afford it.
Men and women sell their bodies for one
    night's food and shelter.
Children run guns and drugs for the clothes
    they wear in gang colors.
Students sign their lives away in hopes of
    getting the extra edge to make it.
Only a certain amount of people have the real
    money.
Pity they don't share it a little more.

Epitaph of the Twentieth Century

People starved, children died
Soldiers fought, widows cried
For love or money on we went.
Our resources were all but spent.
Generation X rebelled.
By Baby Boomers they were quelled.
Communism rose and fell.
"Nazi villains, rot in Hell!"
Africa was in turmoil.
Erosion took away topsoil.
The beat '50's and all that jazz
The '60s added more pizzazz.
Everybody cried and whined.
Celebrities were wined and dined.
Education took a dip.
We saw a resurge of hip.
Television and the King
And other rock stars who can't sing
America had fifty states.
Politicians had debates.
China led by Chairman Mao
Forgot the wisdom of the Tao.
Everybody was depressed
By false memories repressed.
Diplomacy was all in vain.

Classicism on the wane
Neil Armstrong on the moon
Medicare proved quite a boon.
Industrialist Japan
Despite Godzilla and Rodan
Pro athletes strived to win the game
Stage and screen stars all sought fame.
Germany was reunited.
Immigrants came uninvited.
Babble on the radio
Music on a video
Women had the right to vote
Richard Nixon was a goat.
Population ever rising
Businesses began downsizing.
The shuttle was launched into space.
Everybody saving face.
Sweet town Chicago built the Loop.
"Chat with the McLaughlin Group."
"Buy your clothes at Marshall Fields."
"Buy stock on perspective yields."
Drugs and gangs cause lots of crime.
Cities filled with trash and grime.
Whales washed up on the shore.
Tax collectors taking more.
"Are ya feelin' lucky, punk?"
Bag ladies collected junk.
Ford started selling motorcars.
Hollywood was filled with stars.
FDR had a New Deal.
Salesmen spouted their spiel.

Animals became extinct.
The fine line became less distinct.
Philosophers were far and few.
Lie detectors told us what was true.
There's much more; it can't be denied.
What can we say except, "WE TRIED!"

Summer in Chicago

Buildings of every size reflect the sun and
      provide shade for the people on the go.
The roar of cars and rattle of trains provide
      harmony for the stereos and radios.
Salty meats, sugary chocolate, park flowers
      and diesel exhaust perfume the air.
Banners and signs wave in the breezes off the
      lake,
Or sail by on buses and trucks.
Everywhere the people come and go:
Tourists, students, workers of every collar,
      cops, bums, everyday people.
Anywhere you want, you can go.
Anyplace you want to see, anything you want
      to do is a cab ride away.
Tourists stream from museums,
Fans from the stadiums,
Shoppers from the stores.
People from all over make their homes here:
A U.N. without the politics.
Sails of all colors carry boats around on the
      lake,
Frisbees sail back and forth on Oak St. Beach.
Picnics and playgrounds orbit Buckingham
      Fountain in Grant Park.

Odd sculptures adorn the neighborhoods.
The Loop encircles Downtown.
Airplanes coast overhead to and from Midway
and O'hare.
The sound of children's laughter mingles with
the carnival music of Navy Pier.
Bridges of all designs stretch over the river.
Starving musicians sing for their supper.
Worshippers of every creed chant prayers and
blessings in the name of their gods.
While the Sears Tower* reigns as king over the
Greatest City in the World.

---

* This poem was written prior to the 2009 name change to WillisTower.

Glitzville

Hooray for Hollywood
That golden glitter town of Hollywood
Where anything you see or feel
Is never real
It's just all part of the set
Where any act or gag
Has a price tag
You just take what you can get
Where your claim to fame
Is dropping names
But no one cares who you are
Because only money matters
So if you're in tatters
Don't think you'll get very far
So go and do your thing
If you can dance or sing
Hooray for Hollywood

Lament

I weep not for those who have died
But for those who never lived

They that speed through lift so determined to
      get ahead
They never stop to examine or admire the
      scenery as they whisk by
En route to one of their many destinations
They are breathless and weary when the race
      is over

Also they that crawl along through one year
      after the next
Stopping only when they reach their graves
They are stooped with many cares and
      borrowed burdens
So they never look up to return the smile of the
      Man in the Moon

Also for those who shut the world away
Afraid of the sun and streets
Refusing to answer any knock at the door
They are so concerned with keeping out pain
That they shut out joy as well

All of these have been given a precious gift
And they choose to waste it
Because of that, I shed my tears

Wanderlust

Shackled to my present state by worldly
      concerns,
My soul yearns to touch new vistas.
Desert sands, savannah grasses, cobbled
      highways,
All these pathways beckon to me.
The rolling hill of the prairie lands point to the
      Great Western Shore
The rivers and roads of the East bind the cities
      together.

Even the Motherlands of the Old World call to
      me.
The moors of Britain, the plains of the
      Mediterranean, and the mountain forests
      of Slav and Teuton lands draw me to
      Europe.
The mystery and majesty of the Orient dance
      in my dreams
The driest desert and the wettest jungle of
      Africa call out the challenge of survival.
Even as the ranges and rain forests of South
      America echo the cry,

Harmonizing with the great reefs and
    grasslands of the Australian country-
    continent.

Kind daughter-servants of Hestia,
I must bid thee adieu,
And satisfy my longing spirit
Which flies the globe with wandering Hermes

Total Virginity

No sex
No smoking
No drugs
No alcohol
No gambling
No shoplifting

No abortions
No unwanted pregnancies
No venereal diseases
No cancer treatments
No needle scars
No liver damage
No flashbacks
No blackouts
No hitting bottom
No begging or borrowing
No trouble with the law
No hurting friends and family
No broken Commandments

I will not betray God by committing adultery.
I will not poison my body and soul with the
     false pleasures of drugs, tobacco, or
     alcohol.
I will not scar or stain my flesh.
I will not cheapen myself by chasing easy
     money

Instead I will keep myself as pure as I can.
So that when Gabriel calls me home,
I can pass by Michael to the Great Throne and
     say,
"I am as You made me.
Never did I seek to sully the beauty of Your
     Creation."

Petrization

A globe is not a model of the Earth.
It is a picture of the Earth in one brief instant
     of time.
The Earth is not constant.
Its winds and waters shape and reshape its
     features.
The sun both gives life and brings death to the
     many plants and animals
Much like the people who shave away the
     wilderness to make farms and factories.
The fires within the rocks raise mountains and
     sink valleys
Even in Space the Earth does not stand still,
But moves and changes with every moment.

Digital Handcuff

Our world is ordered by its turning around the
     sun
The hands of the clock tack and measure this
     journey
But now so many ask, "What time is it?"
Rather than "What is Time?"
Everything in our lives is ruled by a schedule
We attempt to impose our own order on what
     exists in simple nature
Anything not fitting that order is frowned
     upon
We must always know when we are so we can
     work The Plan
We are fettered by our own ignorance
Trapped in our own labyrinth
With no way back and no way out
We plunge on ahead
Always checking our watches
Determined not to be late

La Philosophette

Everyone knows who she is,
But nobody knows her.
Behind the eyes of her yet young body shines
    an ancient soul.
Though she speaks but rarely,
Her words fall like pearls.
She weaves faith and fact
Into a beautiful tapestry of meaning

Quest D'Amour

When you're looking for someone special
And you keep looking and looking and looking
Vowing to never give up
You just keep on looking
Until you've searched to the ends of the earth

Despairing of ever finding them
The exhaustion forces you to sit down
Then just when you're ready to give up all
        hope
As if by magic, they find you

Spiritual Dystrophy

There's a fog in my brain,
And I can't shake it out.
It's clouded my faith
With the shadows of doubt.
Glitter, glitter everywhere
Yet none of it is gold.
Glitter, glitter everywhere
Just so much dust and mold
I have begun to die inside
The disease is very real
There is no pain; there is no hurt.
I can no longer feel.
From the core inside on out,
My flesh turns into stone.
Growing ever harder more
Than the stiffest brand of bone
My heart beats on within my breast,
An automatous machine.
My mind feels like a lump of lead.
What does all this mean?
All I see are images,
And none of them are real.
They have no substance and no depth,
I touch, but do not feel.
The foil's soft and supple.
The metal's hard and cold.
Glitter, glitter everywhere,
And none of it is gold.

The Ghost of Agnes Edna

She had few friends in her life
And fewer still in death
None but the clock took care to mark
When she drew her final breath
No one cried and no one cared
When she was laid to rest
She had been a mystery
To those who knew her best
Laden down with loneliness
Her soul was filled with grief
Departure from her earthly form
Did not bring it relief
She goes about her daily ways
Just like she did before
The only difference now is that
She doesn't use a door.
Barred from the eternal rest
She has returned to haunt
Those who when she was alive
Accustomed her to taunt
Sometimes you can hear her footsteps
Bringing with them strife.
She comes and goes most quietly
The way she did in life
Of all the demons that we fear
The one I dread the most
Is the melancholy dismal form
Of Agnes Edna's ghost

The Original Dysfunctional Family

Two brothers torn apart
By one woman's jealous heart.
Too young to understand such things,
They will sire a race of kings
Two brothers, full of love,
Brothers blessed by God above

Two women young and old
One of silver, one of gold
One begot the first-born son
The other ranked as number one

One man, husband, father, chief
His wife gave him no relief:
"I will have no joint heirs to the throne.
My son will rule the tribe alone."
Poor man, his heart cleft in twain,
Bleeding with the grief and pain,
To see two brothers torn apart
By one woman's jealous heart.

Leah's Best Son

She's the one whom most forget
Six Hebrew tribes she did beget
Her husband looked on her with scorn
And unto her a son was born
Five more followed and a girl
Each one, to her, a precious pearl
The eldest three met with disgrace
Judah only did save face
Judah's living sons were three
Number two most interests me
His Moabite daughter-in-law Ruth
Had a great-grandson, most famous youth
David, chosen to be King
Much strife and tears his life did bring
David's brood were claimed by Death
All, save the one from Nazareth
He battled Death, most strong and brave
That us from Sin, He would then save
Great Son of Jacob's hated wife
Lead us to Eternal Life

Adolescent Eulogy

The thing that I'll remember
Is the scent she always wore.
Behind her ears and on her wrists
Since she was only four

At Halloween when every girl
Was a witch upon a broom
I always could tell who she was
By smelling her perfume

We didn't always get along
We fought a lot at ten
For days she wouldn't speak to me
I loved her even then

I once wore her perfume home
After the eighth grade dance
It had been such a lovely night
So filled with young romance

Time went by and we grew up
Each year more apart
I didn't know until too late
The weakness of her heart

Today we lay her down to rest
And grieve more for her absence
I'll always carry in my soul
The memory of her fragrance

Storytime

Did I tell you of the Woman
Who lives within a Shell?
If you can only coax her out,
What tales she can tell.

She lives in the Underground
Deep within the Earth.
And she has lived there five thousand years
Ever since her birth.

She has traveled far and wide
And seen many great and wondrous things
If you listen carefully
You can hear the songs she sings

I met her once ten years ago
On a dark and dreary day
I was walking in the woods
And I had lost my way.

She took my hand and led me along
Into her underground home
It was neatly tucked away
Snug in a crystal dome

She told me many fantastic tales
Of a dragon and a prince
Although I've often looked for her
I have not seen her since

You cannot find her when you want
She must come to you
But if she does you will believe
Each word she says is true.

Chained to a Perch

My mother asked me if I would mind running
     an errand for her
So I got in the car and drove to White Hen

The store sits at the crossroads
The northbound street calls me to the great
     Windy City
Even as its southbound twin offers to take me
     to the City of the Dark Poets
My right foot steps towards the East
To the very beginnings of Americana
While my left foot draws me to the West
To virgin wildlands unspoiled by human touch

It would be so easy to just keep going till I can
     go no more
Finding new roads when the old ones end

But Mom needs a gallon of milk
As the Good Daughter I must obey
Till I leave the nest and fly away

Black Roses

Flowers of love, flowers of death
Cut down in their prime
Flowers for my very best friend
Who died before her time
She was driving to the village park
To meet her man with a picnic basket
Now she's laid out before us all
So pretty in her casket
The cabbie who hit her was drunk
Going eight-five miles an hour
Out of control for the roads were wet
With rain from a recent shower
She had barely just begun to bloom
A yet unopened bud
Trampled down by a cruel machine
All wrangled in the mud
We've come to pay her tribute with
These roses painted black
And when I see the flowers grow
I'll always wish her back

Meditations on Turning Twenty

Too young for a woman
Too old for a girl
Lost on my own
In this great big world
My body says one thing
My mind says another
My heart is divided
Between one and the other.
I've been a good girl,
As best I know how.
And I can't help but wonder,
So what happens now?
I'm still not quite ready,
To enter real life.
Will I die an old maid,
Or somebody's ex-wife?
At the same time I hope,
It'll work out for the best;
And I'll be able to set,
All my old fears to rest.
Will the Bible and Rilke
Help me to the end?
Or should I cultivate

A few good close friends?
Another decade is over,
And a new one begins.
Have I been forgiven
Of all my past sins?
I don't know what I'll face,
As I walk through this land,
I can only take hold of God's guiding Hand.

Nightflight

I wish I could step through the window
And be carries away by the wind
To glide over field and forest
Weave through the mountains and valleys
Cross seas and oceans without getting wet
Passing farmhouse and factory
Through city and country
With the owls and nightingales for company
Feeling the breezes blow away my worries
Far away from the screams and dreams of the
     ground
Pushing up through the clouds
To dance with the moon amongst the stars

Karefree Kingdom

How I wish we could escape from ourselves
And go to the land of fairies and elves
Run a race on a plain with a young unicorn
Then dance to the tune of the dwarfly pipehorn
Take a dip with the mermaids in the Great
     Crystal Sea
Or fly with the Phoenix so high and so free
Play on a meadow where the rose never wilts
Then sleep on a mountain where the clouds
     serve as quilts
Sing 'round a fire with brave knights and
     mages
And not care about the work-world of wages
This magnificent realm sits between the bright
     stars
And if we close our eyes, it can be just all ours

Mr. Dee-Jay

He's the closest thing to a man in my life.
We wade through the lonely hours of the night
     together
Reaching our over the airwaves
Without ever seeing each other's faces
He tells me the news and the weather
     sometimes
But mostly he just plays the songs my soul
     dances to
We skip around three decades of music
Mixing tender ballads and jazzy ditties
Some have to be cranked up
Others heard softly as whispers
Loyal to him I don't change my dial
And sometimes I'll even sing along for awhile

Plea to Apollo

Sing while you plat, o great virtuoso!
As you said to Marsayas some dark days ago.
Sing while you play on you're beautiful lyre,
And let me be warmed by your musical fire.
Sing while you play, one note do not miss
And I shall reward thee with a most thankful
     kiss.
Sing while you play, you Greek god of stone.
Sing about friendship, so I won't feel alone.
Sing while you play, Latona's second-born,
While I sit at your feet, quite lost and forlorn
Sing while you play, your hands poised to
     strike
Sing while you play any old song that you like.
Sing while you play, o great beautiful statue.
Sing while you play, as I sit gazing at you.

Artemis

Your passions are simple
Your pleasures but two
Your enemies many
Your followers few
Daytime or night
You hunt and you run
As equal an archer
As your brother the sun
When your nymphs play the harp
You dance and you sing
Yet your joy is missing
One great crucial thing
You have no true companion
You have no one t love
Orion, once, maybe
But now he hunts above
But live as you choose
Your path is your own
But ask yourself this,
Can you live all alone?

Requiem for Actaeon

He has gone now
And the candle burns on
Even as the flames of my heart smolder
The sparks were struck by the friction of Lust
     and Blooming Passion
On a pristine plain of Innocence
Fear, holy fear, sounded an alarm
Which rose about the seductive crooning

As though tearing flesh from bone
I pulled away
Trying to stop the flow of my heartblood
The music is silent
And the candle burns on
Dripping wax that mirrors my own tears
I have smelled the heady musk of Desire
And been intoxicated by the fragrance

With trembling breath I blow out the candle
And sit in silent darkness as I have these past
     twenty years
Trying to glue my heart back together
As I weep for memories I never made.

Summer of '89

The was the year that I started to grow,
In the summer of '89.
The body I'd had for eleven years
Was no longer to be mine
I walked around with folded arms,
To cover my growing chest
I was the only girl my age I knew,
Who'd begun to sprout her breasts.
When I ran, I was slowed way down,
But a painfully obvious bounce
My mother told me not to worry:
"It's what inside you that counts."
But she didn't hear the jokes and jeers
Of kids who though they were cool.
I never knew until that year,
That children could be so cruel.
Now that I'm grown and looking back
I think it's so shamefully sad.
What should have been one of my happiest
        years
Was at times so unbearably bad

The One in the Corner

I've seen her around,
But don't know who she is.
I've been too busy,
What with class and the kids.
She's always alone,
With this look on her face.
Her mind's somewhere else,
Like in outer space.
She looks other-worldly.
She seems very wise.
Behind her glasses repose
This bizarre pair of eyes.
They just see what they want,
Or they're totally blind.
I sometimes wonder,
What goes on in her mind?
She just plays along
In the role she's been cast
You just missed her now
You didn't see her go past
She comes and goes quietly
That's just her way.
Maybe I'll talk to her
Later on today.

Knight of Swords, King of Hearts

For twenty years now I've stood on a pedestal
Locked in an ivory tower
With my music and poems, drama and dreams
I passed each lonely hour.
I never saw much of the world outside.
The world they say is real.
And then I met a man of tat world,
And he taught m how to feel.
He swept into my life a refreshing breeze,
And set my emotions churning.
For the first time in two decades and more
I could feel Passion's fire burning.
Like Sleeping Beauty and Snow White,
He roused me with a kiss.
Now my mind is filled with things
I cannot just dismiss.
The veils and curtains have been drawn back.
I can see the light of day.
The door is open; the road is clear
I can go on my own way.

There are many paths and many roads
And I am free to choose
If I follow my heart wherever it leads,
Then there's no way I can lose.
In a year the Man who set me free
Will no doubt forget my name
I will remember forevermore
And I'm grateful all the same.

Starstuff

Tearing my eyes from false light to true,
I return the smile of the Man in the Moon,
Who sits as a jolly eunuch tending all the stars
I don't know which is mine.
There are fewer shining than in days past,
And more are ever flickering
Yet some still glow bright,
And more are kindled with each turn,
Even thought twice as many fall.

And what of their fate?
Some are plucked and tossed into darkness.
Some crash hard upon the earth,
Leaving craters in the soul.
Some are caught, but dropped,
Lost as they extinguish
Yet many are caught by loving hands,
And serve as embers from which Love's glow
        and Passion's heat enflame,
Burning upon the divine hearth.

My stars time to set will come,
But who shall cushion its descent?
Shall I catch his in return?

Windsong

The wind never stops playing its music
It knows only one song of infinite variations
It plays for the rocks, the plants, the animals,
      and for itself
It sings of joy and sorrow
Of love and hate
The sun and moon and stars give the light by
      which it dances on stage
Sometimes it sings to itself
Too soft for mortals to hear
But that ever appreciative audience the angels
      applaud in our stead.

Rainbow Roses

In every generation, Fate sows a few special
      souls
These uniques grow and blossom into
      brilliance
Their colors shed different luster than those
      growing around them
They glow with their own special inner light
They are adored
They are loved
They are shunned
And feared
Too many times these precious blossoms are
      weeded over
The vines rally their strength to choke out the
      alien
Our only hope is that they have time to seed
Before the Gardener plucks them from the
      earth

Nightwalk

The trees don't think I'm crazy for talking to
    myself.
The moon doesn't care if I don't make eye
    contact.
The wind and clouds keep playing their game.
The birds and squirrels give me privacy.
The earth listens with ancient patience.
The sky betrays no undue concern.
For how many before me have paced this path?
Seeking solitude in a Holy Place,
At an hour sacred to the Goddess?
Many have,
And many will.
So truly, I am not alone.

Sundancer

The wind and the water play the same old
     song.
The performer moves as she always has:
Weaving through the spotlight,
She never wavers or pauses,
Dancing for the glory of the Creator
Keeping time to the heartbeat of the universe.

She is but one of many on stage,
Yet no less a part of the Grand Ballet.
Spinning forever, but never dizzy,
She has the grace of the ages.

Bravado

It is easy to perpetuate the façade of bravery.
The boastful lies drop like divers from the lips.
We can even fool ourselves.

Yet whatever our minds believe,
Our bodies know the truth.
The tell-tale heart clicks louder with every
      beat,
And the guts, trained to vent fear, twist about
      as the demons rattle the bars of their
      cages.
The thoughts of deserving hellfire enflame our
      faces
While the chills of fear ripple from the spine.

It is easy to perpetuate the façade of bravery,
And a thousand times harder to veil the truth.

Walking in Winter

Put on my coat and laced my boots
Got ready to go
Stepped out into the Valley of 1,000 Trees
In the middle of the falling snow

The valley's green is gone now
The leaves have all fallen down
The animals have taken cover
But if you look you'll see them scurry around

The little children built a snowman
Then went off to skate on the lake
I used to play for weeks out here
And the memories are more than I can take

Jack Frost came up to me.
He asked, "Do you want to play?"
I said, "I'm too old and sad now.
You should have asked me yesterday."

Walking in winter
Each step takes me further back in time
Walking in winter
Take a rest beneath the tree I used to climb

Typist

Clickedy-clack
    Clickedy-clack
        Clickedy-clack

Fingers dance back and forth across the keys.
Choreographing an impromptu pas de deux
Symbols form on the glowing screen
Linking together to convey a picture
An assortment of idle images and sequences
Pieced together during the lonely hours of the
      night by a dreaming soul
Mind, breath, and body are all focused to the
      task

Clickedy-clack
    Clickedy-clack
        Clickedy-clack

From the Rut Across the Fence

You and me, we come from different worlds.
You get so scared because you don't
        understand my words
You think I'm crazy,
And you wonder why
You hear me laugh a lot, but you've never seen
        me cry.
Well, what else can I say?
I've always lived life this way.

You look at me; you don't know just what to do.
I seem so cheerful, but you know deep down
        I'm blue.
You have your life.
I do my thing.
I like to dance sometimes, but I'm too afraid to
        sing.
Well, what else can I say?
I've always lived life this way

With poems and sketches, with songs and
      books
I hide in places where nobody ever looks
All of my passion
All of my rage
I keep them prisoner in a tightly locked up
      cage.
Well, what else can I say?
I've always lived life this way

Well, what else can I say?
I've always lived life this way
In work, rest, and play,
I do things my own way

Sometimes I wonder, how my life will end?
If I will be alone or surrounded by my friends?
I may go crazy
Then I'll wonder why
If I have never lived, then how is it I can die?
Well, what else can I say?
I've always lived life this way

Riding Amphitrite's Steed

The Pacific sun sends down battering rams of
    heat
Faintly dispelled by the ocean breezes
The gulls have long since left us in silent
    stillness
Save for the soft roar of the waves and the
    chirping notes of his song
In this moment we are more intimate than we
    will ever be
Skating together across the barrier between
    our worlds
No words I can say will tell him this
But he knows and understands
He shows me by his enigmatic perpetual smile
He will leave me at the dock soon
And we will continue through life touched but
    never touching.
Yet for now I can feel his strong body carrying
    me on waves of pleasure
As real as those rising and falling around us
I bend forward and pat his nose
A gesture that means more to us than any
    lovers' kiss

Angelica's Journey

To fly through the black night of space an
       angel must first wait for a star to fall
Saddling the flame she rides to her chosen
       world
The heavenly fires consume her wings
The wandering soul takes root in flesh growing
       as flesh does
Running and smiling
Laughing and dancing
Touching and being touched
Loving and being loved

Yet the wind constantly whispers reminders of
       a greater freedom
Like a blooming flower her burnt wings grow
       anew
Taking new first steps she glides and coasts
Practicing each ancient memory
Until the winds launch her home

Blessed Blend

Man is born from a union of Animal and Angel
An even mixture of soul and soil
The Animal in us dies
While the Angel lives forever
The natures of these parents are as of
      opposites
Spirit and Flesh
Eternal, yet constrained
Free, but fleeting

So often our mixed heritage drives us to self-
      separation
Drawing us nearer to Heaven or Earth
Alienating us from those who are our kin
Causing us to forget that the Creator willed
      this union by the power of Love
Even at Divorce the Angels carry Animal-
      memories in their feathers
May we have the strength not to divide, but to
      reconcile, the twin halves of our Beings.

Cleft in Twain

When I was little I asked my father, "Why are
    there two Germanys?"
He said, "One is Communist. The other is
    Democratic.
They were divided during the war."
I asked him, "Why are there two Irelands?"
He said, "One is a free country. The other
    belongs to Great Britain.
They, too, where divided during a war."
That didn't sound right to me.
I thought there should be one Germany, one
    Ireland.
Then I grew up, and a wall came a 'tumbling
    down
Now there is one Germany and two Irelands
Perhaps when I grow older there will be one
    Ireland
One nation, under God, indivisible

Radio Rambling

Tell me the news, yes.
Read me the scores and temperatures.
Let me know how the traffic is.
And be sure to remind me about live
        broadcasts and contest giveaways

But most of all play the music
Old sad ballads
New hip-hop dance mixes
Jazzy blues
And gangsta rap
Men and women sing about heartache and new
        love
Songs that have flared into flame only to burn
        out
Let me add my voices to theirs
Joining in the grand chorus of they who can
        sing never to be heard.

Hey Maestro

Play me those same old riffs
That old familiar rhythm that echoes in my
      bones
Don't worry about the words
My heart remembers what the charts forget
The meaning doesn't matter anyway
Just sing me the sounds
So I get lost in a maze of melody

Ponder the lyrics the way you look for wisdom
      in an abstract painting
Fathom the artist's philosophy if you want
I'd rather just stare at the images
Until the colors blend into a rainbow
And the shapes unshape themselves.

Seeker's Sojourn

Every morn I see the sun rise o'er the land
Wind blows the fog away with mighty breath
And every second light conquers the darkness
Just as the Holy Son triumphed over Death

Each day brings a new way, a new chance
Just as the road brings on another turn
I must select the path that I will follow
Watching while the guiding lights still burn

Each choice brings a consequence I know
I trust my faith will pick the one that's best
The sun grows bright, the day grows hot
      around me
But I keep walking towards Eternal Rest

The road comes to an end before my feet
In the place where the Earth meets with the
      sky
Instead of legs, white wings spread forth
      around me
Hands push me up and far away I fly

O Brother, Christ, my Brother
Walk with me now
Please take my hand
O Father, God my Father
Please guide my way
Across the land
Walk with me and hold my hand

Catharsis

A dragon breathes flames so that the fires of
     his heart will not consume him from the
     inside.
These flames ride hidden in the wind and find
     other hearts in which to burn
Such is how humans share in the passion
     power of the dragon

But to a heart frozen by loneliness and despair
Which pumps blood from habit than happiness
The warmth of a touch can sting
To the unaccustomed passion's fire blinds and
     blisters
The grim beauty of the dragon awes us so that
     we flee in terror from the flames
It is too easy to sit in the darkened cold
Becoming numb statues waiting for death to
     crumble us

It takes more courage to approach the flame
To watch it dance displaying its strength
Inviting us to draw out of our ice caves
And roam the world as the dragon roams the
     sky

Frater de Espiritu

Come with me to the river
Where we can cleanse our souls
And mend our ragged reputations
Worn with rents and holes
I've heard others talk of you
But they speak not the truth
I see differently than they
I see a pleasant, handsome youth
And so I drew near unto you
In you I can confide
With others I must wear a mask
With you I need not hide
Between us we can share so much
And need not be afraid
What's said between us stays between us
So that neither is betrayed
We accept and understand
We don't condemn or judge
We speak our minds quite openly
We don't hold a silent grudge
The road of live divides for us
We'll go off in different lanes
But the bond we share endures forever
And never fades or wanes
And when we die, wherever we are
In the grip of fire or ice
Our Father will bring us together again
United in His Paradise

Devil's Brew

The road to Margaritaville is paved with
    frustration.
Its soft lights are welcome to eyes strained by
    sun and storm
Its walls offer shelter against wind and worry
And friendly locals offer a golden elixir to
    chase away the aches and pains of the
    world.

Drink to celebrate
Drink to forget
Drink to quench your thirst

Yet there is poison in the potion
A dark poison that harms but little when little
But grows in strength like the roots of a weed
As the potion wears off, the poison begins to
    kill
Attacking body, mind and spirit together at
    once.
Made from fruits and grains grown in God's
    own garden
Yet it is Lucifer's own creation
For those killed by this poison are surely slain
    by his hand
In offering Happiness he brings Death
As he has done since Eden

Why I Cannot Drink

Yes, I have tasted beer
And whiskey and wine and all other such
In each I have tasted bitterness
The bitterness that awaits me at the bottom of
      the glass
For each drink chips away at the seal
The seal that imprisons my demons
I do not know the strength of that seal
So I would be a fool to weaken it.
Let the demons writhe in their cage
Let them howl with thirst
I will not set them free.
I will not give them drink.
My Brother warns against it
My Father hath forbid it
Temptation dance round me
Though his efforts are in vain
Let the demons how in thirst
I will not give them drink

Clouds Over London

People are herded together in houses and
      blocks
With only streets and tubes to give them
      motion
Even they are bound
Prisoners manacled by time
Jailed by their own proclivity
The wilderness that once claimed this place is
      tamed into parks and gardens
Even the birds, slaves to hunger, may only fly
      where there is food
Only the clouds are truly free.
They glide overhead skating on the wind
Holding or dropping rain as they please
Skipping on parade before the sun
Answering only to their Creator

Midnight in Mayfair

The sun has long since gone down on me
The stars are dimmed by the streetlamps
Though this city never sleeps it has gone to
      bed.
But though I walk in dark places and passages
      of no light I am not afraid
Should I be afraid when I am not alone?
My Father watches over me
My Brother walks beside me
My guides and guardians lead and follow
Ready to catch me if I fall
Or carry me when I tire
Wherever I go they come along
Whenever I travel, they do not leave me
Though I am far from home they are with me
      always
I need not see their shadows
I do not listen for their footsteps
I know in my heart they are there
And that faith draws them even closer

In Trafalgar Square

Admiral Nelson gazes toward the seas as if
    remembering his faraway deathbed
A defeat in victory memorialized for all time
A tyrant beaten down for the safety and
    freedom of those who go about the square
The people who sit and smile and take pictures
The children who climb and chase

Children, do not chase after the pigeons like
    hunting cats
They will not come but will fly farther faster
    than you can run
Rather be still and patient
Then they will see you mean no harm
Offer them food in the ancient gesture of
    welcome
Soon they will not fear to eat from your hands

Remember too that they are God's creatures
Though not formed in His image their wings
    are modeled after the angels'

Wish You Were Here

The wind sets the flowers dancing
And carries their perfume through the air
Soft clouds march on parade before the sun
Birds sing praises in thanks for the day
All the little animals come out to play
But what good is paradise when you're alone?

Waves softly caress the beach
Stones and shells sparkle like gems
Gulls glide about alongside kites
The water offers refreshment from sorrow
Telling me not to fear for tomorrow
But what good is paradise when you're alone?

Mountains stand guard flanking the lush
    valley
Trees offer gifts of sweet fruit
Green grass carpets this outdoor banquet hall
Nature's gentility, not at all rough
If this is not Eden, well then, close enough
But what good is paradise when you're alone?

Dolor de Corazon

Clothes and shoes I remembered to pack
But I left my heart behind
Walkman and tapes in my carryon sack
But I left my heart behind
All reservations have been confirmed
Yet I left my heart behind
Library books are all returned
Yet I left my heart behind
I have money and tickets and all that I need
I just left my heart behind
My plants and my pets I arranged to feed
I just left my heart behind
I waited so long to take this trip
And I left my heart behind
I'll be away for months at a clip
And I left my heart behind

All I can do is board the plane
And then be ready to fly
Telling myself that I'll be okay
And wishing I knew how to cry
Music plays but all I can hear
Is the song to which we danced

Why didn't I speak up before
When I still had the chance
Now I won't see him for a long long time
Perhaps not till next year
Will he find someone to take my place
That is my nightmare
I don't know what will happen when I return
I don't know what I will find
But the next time I must go away
I won't leave my heart behind.

Fountain's Abbey

Your stones have stood the test of time
For almost a thousand years
O'er you the monks who lived here once
Cried long and bitter tears
Stripped down by a greedy king
A man of gold not God
Now tourists boldly photograph
The paths your inmates trod
A beauteous place you once stood proud
A sacred house of prayer
Now giftshops, restaurants and tours
Replace your chapel square
The Fountains Abbey bells are silent
Nevermore to toll
But pack a lunch and spend the day
And take a country stroll.

Edinburgh

Bonnie dear ol' Scotlandtown
On hills both high and low
Castles loom in majesty
O'er people on the go
Friendly faces, pretty places
Everywhere you turn
Lovely lasses, bonnie lads
And something new to learn
Pour the whiskey on and dance
To sweet old bagpipe songs
Kick your heels up and prance
Rejoice the whole year long
History lives within these walls
Growing more each day
Scholars and soldiers gather here
Going on their bonnie way
From the old clan patriarchs
To the very youngest tots
A home away from home to me
Is the dear town of the Scots

On the North Sea Shore

The wind and sea reach out to touch
On shores I cannot name.
How many sailors have stood here once
And felt the water's claim?
So many islands has the Earth
And these upon we live
Sailing from one on to the next,
To see what it will give
Now children play upon this beach
And couples come to stroll
Past the surf out to the deep
The waves forever roll
The cliffs have stood in silent witness
To watch each year go by
And clouds roll on as they always have
In their playground called the sky
Two nations touch upon this shore,
Two different peoples meet.
Here cold dark Ran, the goddess Norse,
Must once have held her seat.
Sometime I'll come back to this place,
But not just for the day
I'll build a boat, cast anchor off,
And sail far away.

Castle by the Sea

Oh, to live as a lady of days gone by
In a castle by the sea
Far from the pressures and intrigues of court
In a castle by the sea
Banquets and croquet and rides on the beach
In a castle by the sea
The roar of the waves is a soft lullaby
In a castle by the sea
Gulls singing and chirping throughout all the
     year
In a castle by the sea
Some day I'll come with my dear beloved
Together just him and me
And we'll live forever in a world of our own
In a castle by the sea

York Town

Old meets New in the city of York in the heart
of its namesake shire
From a Gothic cathedral to cobblestone streets
there is much in this town to admire
Ghosts too dwell within these walls in every
place and age
Bound in torment by their passion, cursed
because of rage
Street performers give their shows each
different every day
At night drink at the King's Cross Pub while
swans swim on their way
Anything at all you want can be found in the
market streets
Clothes and jewels and souvenirs, lemonades,
books, and sweets
History buffs explore the past with no end of
delight
Lots of fun for everyone in the land of roses
white

River Ouse

You've seen the Romans come and go,
And quietly ever on you flow.
The Normans came and beat the Danes,
But you cared not for all their pains.
The Brits and Scots have warred here oft,
And still you rustle ever soft.
You in this town alone will last.
You have witnessed all its past.
On your banks people rush and hurry,
But their concern is not your worry.
You flow on reaching toward the sea,
Content for always just to be.

Las Souers Bronte

Yorkshire Muses, sisters three, in a country
      parson home
Upon the moors among the ghosts, this trio
      loved to roam
Last of their siblings, like their pens, they
      have laid down to rest
But while they held these poet's tools they
      gave their very best
Pioneers of literature in Victoria's golden reign
The all told of the truth of life its passion and
      its pain
Departed now to a higher kingdom with
      streets all paved with gold
In their stories we remember them each time
      each one is told

Longing

The half-moon grins down on Windermere lake
I wonder if you're watching it smile
Land and ocean span out between us
Stretching mile upon mile
It's after lunchtime now where you are
Soon you'll be out with your friends
Tonight I will dream on in loneliness
And a sorrow that never quite ends

Avon

Swans and geese and ducks galore parade
    among the boats
The willows all along the shore show off their
    emerald coats
Bisecting the heart of Shakespeareland, proud
    rival to the Thames
Sparkles of sunshine on the surface glitter like
    gleaming gems
Never once held prisoner in the shackling
    chains of ice
Always free to flow forever careless of men and
    mice
A ribbon of beauty, a haven of life with glory
    on every side
The River Avon rustles on as Stratford's
    second pride.

Dover

Sailing away from the white cliffs of Dover
How many have bid them farewell?
How much have they seen and if they could
    talk,
What tales would they have to tell?
Of the vast legionnaires who came up from
    Gaul
For the Empire's reach to expand?
Of the Angles and Saxons who conquered the
    Brits
And gave a new name to the land?
Of the French and the English who fought
    back and forth
When two crowns were claimed by one man?
Of the mighty Armada, despite arrogant
    boasts,
Turned from the battle and ran?
How many ships have come safe to port?
How many lie sunk in the deep?
The white cliffs of Dover, they answer me not.
What secrets they have, they will keep.

Impressions of a Carnival

As the sun goes down, the volume goes up
Families walk their little ones home
Time for the big kids to come out and play
Nectar and ambrosia flow freely.
The stars are outshined by a rainbow of
　　　flashing flares
A wild plush menagerie dances among the
　　　revelers
The music echoes the passions dancing in the
　　　breezes
Spirits soar alongside the fireworks
All dark in heart feel the magic in the air
Dancing and laughing without the weight of
　　　care

Jay

When I think of him
I think of plaid
Plaid like an old comfy blanket
The kind you wrap up in on some cold rainy
     night
Sitting on an old couch before a roaring fire
Sipping a cup of sweet hot chocolate
Just holding hands with your lover
Not needing to say a word
But just quietly being together

Vertigo

Dancing around on a carousel
Trapped in Time in Space
Music playing, never stopping
Locked within this place
Animals of every nation
Laughing in my face

Faster, slower as I'm moving
All around the floor
Children laughing, parents watching
As they've done before
Now the tune repeats and I can't
Stand it anymore

Looking for a way to get out
Don't know where to turn
The clown who dances with me asks,
"Girl, won't you ever learn?"
Passion now ignites within me
Causing me to burn

Dancing around on a carousel
No one cuts me slack
Music stops and motion ceases
Pausing in its track
Running away, flying free now
Never looking back

Flames

Fire in the heart began it all
Fire in the desolation brought black snow
Fire in the rain brought destruction but not
      death
Fire in the hearth inspired men to fight
Fire in the field brought despair

Fire in the sea changed it all
Fire in the east and west caused people to hide
      in the night
Fire from the sky brought it all to an end
Daring those who survived to play with
      matches.

Not the One

You breezed into my life
You came to steal my soul
When I looked in your eyes
Deep inside I felt cold

When I spent time with you
Something in me would burn
I didn't know what to do
I didn't know where to turn

You're not the one for me.
I can see that now.
I'll move on from here.
I'll survive some how
Since the day we met all you brought me is
        pain.
I'll move on and forget that my love was in
        vain.

Patience

I saw blossoms on a cherry tree
And reveled in their scent
I dreamed that I might taste of them
And thereby be content
I left and then when I returned
The blossoms left were few
The Lord said, "Do not fret, my child.
Such fruit is not for you."

I left the orchard for the grove
Where walnut trees abound
Some still hung upon the boughs
More lay upon the ground
I strove in vain to crack just one
Till effort left me blue
The Lord said, "Do not fret, my child.
Such fruit is not for you."

I made my may then to the brook
A-sighing as I went
I took a drink and told myself,
"With this, I'll be content."

When I looked up, I saw an arbor
Fresh and damp with dew
The Lord said, "Take your fill, my child.
This fruit is all for you."

Kneeling Over Your Grave

I could stand in fire
When you told me to be bold
And with you I reclaimed something I never
      knew I sold

You gave me hope you showed me strength
You taught me how to pray
You changed my life forever on that awesome
      fateful day

Now you're gone
People shake their heads and wonder why
How could someone who reeked of life just
      simply choose to die?

I can't say
And anyway I would not be believed
All that I can tell them is your burden is
      relieved

In the course of time we'll meet again
We'll talk about your fight
We'll walk through shadowed valleys looking
      only at the light

Requiem Artista

You may indeed say I suffer for my art
I lock myself in the studio
Taking neither rest nor refreshment
Racing to capture the glow of a fastly fading
fallen star

I permit none to disturb my labors
Though friends and lovers cry out from a
distance
My ears are deaf to all
Save for the soft whisper of the brush dancing
over the canvass
Their patience burns out
And they leave
No reason to cry
And yet my tears somehow thin the paint

I have the shallow glory of fame
But the applause is not for ME
Only for the daubed signature in the lower
right-hand corner

Some years hence I will turn from painting to
sculpture
And create one last magnum opus
For I can trust no one else to carve my
tombstone

Modern Science

Scientists tell us that the gases in the
      atmosphere distort and refract the light
      produced by the combustion of the sun's
      helium core.
They can't just say it's a pretty sunset?

Scientists tell us that fertilization causes the
      flower to shed its petals as the pistil
      swells and fills with carbohydrate flesh.
They can't just eat the apple in peace?

Scientists tell us that the sounds we hear are
      actually the vibrations of a string or
      surface that has been plucked or struck.
They can't just listen to the music?

Scientists tell us that certain chemicals trigger
      a response in the olfactory lobes of the
      brain.
They can't just stop and smell the roses?

Scientists tell us that the changing of
      pressures on the skin trigger a nervous
      chain reaction producing a pleasurable
      feeling.
They can't just sit back and relax?

Scientists tell us that billions of years from
      now our sun will go nova ending life on
      this planet.
They can't just cross that bridge when they
      come to it?

Scientists can produce a clone, defeat the pull
      of gravity, split the atom, create a virus,
      and link the entire world via satellites
      and phone lines.
Can they see the flip side of the coin?

Are scientists wrong?

Are scientists right?

Puddle

What a thing of beauty is a puddle
How free in form
How natural in content
In shape and placement how random and
      spontaneous
In reflection how like a mirror
In expression how like a dream.

The Gathering of Water

Mississippi's flowing low tonight
On past Memphis all lit up so bright
River's going where it has to be
Under the bridges out into the sea
The river's golden with the setting sun
All the worries of the day are done
Stars are coming out to fill the sky
Silver bird is taking off to fly
Work is over and it's time to dance
Old Mississippi's got me in a trance
Ride the current going slowly south
All the way to the River's mouth
Past the Gulf and then I'm floating free
Crystal clear Caribbean Sea

Afterword

I hadn't realized just how prolific a poet I had been until I started sorting through them trying to pick the wheat from the chaff. I was surprised to discover that when everything was tallied, the rhyming poems were in the minority. I'd always taken comfort in the structure of the rhyming forms even though it would sometimes take hours or days to find just the right word.

Since leaving college my creative energies have been more focused on prose. So much so that for a time I'd lost my poetic voice, and I hadn't even noticed. As I was compiling this book I worried these would be the last poems I'd ever write.

And then, just when I'd made peace with the fact that my muse had left me, it came back. It returned when my mind was focused on something else, and like that evening on the bridge in Chicago I found myself scrambling for pen and paper.

Hopefully in the years to come I will have more such moments. For now I hope you the reader have enjoyed my versifications. Thank you.

--Lauren Cidell
February 29,2016

www.ingramcontent.com/pod-product-compliance
Lightning Source LLC
Chambersburg PA
CBHW031552040426
42452CB00006B/286